P

CROSSING DIVIDES

"*Crossing Divides* documents a journey from the Hudson to Standing Rock on the banks of the Missouri River, where Vernon Benjamin delivered supplies to Indigenous protesters opposing construction of an oil pipeline they feared would desecrate and contaminate their ancestral land and waters. Benjamin's account of his trip into the heart of the Lakota encampment is wrapped in his own personal story – journalist, political leader, academic, friend to New York's Mohawk Nation, and activist. This is a little book with a big heart."

–Ned Sullivan, President, Scenic Hudson

"Vernon Benjamin meant a lot to me as a friend, mentor, and devoted citizen of Saugerties. He wrote the definitive history of the Hudson River Valley. Late in life he also wrote this account of his trip to Standing Rock to help protesters trying to stop an oil pipeline. In this book we get the essence of Vernon – his deep feelings for history and Native Americans, his years of work for the environment, even his self-doubts. Read this book and meet a remarkable man."

"Vernon Benjamin was one of those special people in our community: journalist, public official, historian, supporter of good causes, and friend, especially a friend. Yet at 70 he drove west to the Standing Rock protests. This book is a powerful testament to the fact that we're never too old to fight against injustices. Or to learn new things about ourselves. In not many pages Vernon Benjamin tells a sweeping story about what it means to care about history and all of us caught in these tumultuous times. This is a little gem of a book I won't forget anytime soon."

CROSSING DIVIDES

MY JOURNEY TO STANDING ROCK

VERNON BENJAMIN

Crossing Divides: My Journey to Standing Rock by Vernon Benjamin
© 2023 Stacey Butcher and Rachel Bingham

"Introduction" and "Vernon Benjamin: A Life"
Copyright © 2023 Will Nixon
Published by Bushwhack Books • Woodstock, NY

Photo credits: Josue Rivas, Standing Rock photo. Mike Saporito, front and back cover author portrait & Vernon Benjamin: A Life 1980s photo. All other photos from author's family archive.

Cover and interior book design by Jessika Hazelton
The Troy Book Makers • Troy, New York • thetroybookmakers.com

Printed in the United States of America

ISBN: 978-0-9886398-7-4

CONTENTS

INTRODUCTION

Here in the Hudson Valley we may live far from the classic oil patch — no pumpjacks rocking up and down, no pipelines snaking through the land — but the fracking boom that began around 2008 brought this business close to home. Ever since the first oil strike in Pennsylvania in 1859, drillers had tapped underground pools and reservoirs. Now the new technology of hydraulic fracturing enabled them to pump water, sand, and chemicals into underground shale beds that fractured and released oil and gas from the sedimentary rock. This industry flourished in North Dakota, Texas, and Pennsylvania. Since the Marcellus Shale formation laden with natural gas stretches from West Virginia through Pennsylvania far into New York, here in the Hudson Valley we feared that drilling pads might soon show up in our own fields and forests. *Gasland*, a documentary filmed partly in Pennsylvania, showed a man holding a lighter to the tap water from his sink faucet until the water, contaminated by methane, burst into flame. Not just our drinking water, but our rivers and creeks, our natural habitats, our very health and safely felt threatened. "Ban Fracking" became the mantra on bumper stickers and lawn signs. In 2014, Governor Andrew Cuomo did, indeed, ban fracking in New York as a public health threat.

But we weren't done with the fracking boom. That same year oil trains began running through the Hudson Valley, mile-long strings of black tanker cars on tracks that hug the shoreline, cross old bridges, and cut through cities, towns, and villages. A potential oil spill on wheels. They came from North Dakota, where the fracking industry spread so rapidly across the Bakken Shale formation that the necessary pipelines hadn't yet been built. So the shale oil got loaded onto trains bound for refineries in New Jersey or Philadelphia. The danger was that this shale oil included other compounds far more volatile than the oil itself. One night in Lac-Megantic, Quebec an untended train left parked on a rise rolled into town, derailed, exploded, and killed forty-seven people. Dubbed "bomb trains" these rolling pipelines were an unnerving sight to those of us stopped in our cars behind railroad crossing gates, where we could feel the rumbling might of the oil empire rushing heedlessly towards global warming.

The industry proposed an alternative to the oil trains as well as the barges transporting fracked oil down the Hudson River: a pair of pipelines to run south of Albany beside the New York State Thruway. Great opposition arose to plans for this Pilgrim Pipeline, and in the end industry built pipelines directly out of North Dakota to reduce the need for the trains.

The biggest battles were out West. The most famous targeted the proposed Keystone XL pipeline, part of a network that connected the oil sands in Alberta, Canada to refineries on the Gulf Coast in Texas. The main sections of the system got built without controversy. But not the Keystone XL which would provide a shortcut through Montana, South Dakota, and Nebraska. Two protests at the White House introduced many of us to pipeline politics for the first time. In August 2011, 1,200 people got arrested, including Bill McKibben, who described this event as "the biggest civil disobedience action in the environmental movement in many years." In November upwards of 12,000 people circled the White House, chanting "Hey Obama, we don't want no climate drama!" This campaign brought together Native Americans defending tribal lands, farmers protecting water resources, and climate activists young and old who wanted to take bold action. And they succeeded. President Barack Obama blocked the project in 2015. President Joe Biden killed it in 2021.

In the shadow of the Keystone XL battle came the fight over the Dakota Access Pipeline to be built from North Dakota to Illinois. In 2014, the Army Corps of Engineers rerouted the proposed pipeline from north of Bismarck, the state capital, to north of the Standing Rock reservation, the poorest corner of North Dakota. In April 2016, as construction began on this 1,172-mile-long project, a small group of Sioux "Water Protectors" set up a protest camp in the grassy knolls by the Missouri River, one of the few crossings for which the Army Corps hadn't yet issued a permit. Gradually, the Water Protectors drew public attention. In July, thirty-six young Indigenous runners completed a 2,000-mile relay to deliver 160,000 signatures to the White House and the Army Corps of Engineers. Standing Rock became a national fight like Keystone.

That summer and fall so many supporters arrived that a second camp was established and followed by several satellite outposts. At their peak 10,000 people lived in these temporary villages. For the Sioux and other tribes, Standing Rock felt like a spiritual and cultural renewal, the largest, most unified gathering of Native Americans in a century and a half. More than 300 Indigenous national flags flew in a half-mile-long row in the central camp. A council fire was tended 24/7. Communal kitchens kept corn and soup simmering in pots. A day school was set up for children. There were bonfires at night, prayers at dawn. As Nick Estes writes in his book, *Our History Is the Future*, "When there was an action planned for the day, an Eyapaha [town crier] rode through the camp on a bicycle, a horse, or in the back of a pickup rousing people from slumber, 'You didn't come here to sleep. This ain't a vacation. We came here to stop a pipeline!'"

The protests were peaceful, but tensions built. The pipeline was rapidly being constructed everywhere else, leaving a gap at the Missouri River as the sore point for the company. The battle was waged in the courts, where judges issued temporary decisions that shifted the momentum back and forth. (In the end Donald Trump was elected president and quickly overrode the objections. In May 2017 oil began flowing through the finished pipeline.)

In September 2016, three bulldozers had arrived to plow two miles of land for the pipeline corridor the day after an archaeologist told a court that burial sites had been found on this land. Enraged protesters ripped down a chain link fence to be met by pepper spray and attack dogs. News images reminiscent of police dogs attacking civil rights protesters in the 1960s sparked outrage. But the violence had started.

The pipeline company hired a security firm, TigerSwan, that had worked in Afghanistan and Iraq and now coordinated with police and the National Guard. They monitored protesters on social media and sent disruptive infiltrators into the camps. In October, the police in riot masks and bulletproof vests, backed by armored ve-hicles, cleared a smaller camp in a scene like a war zone: helicopters circled overhead, sound cannons blared, rubber bullets flew. The arrested were held overnight in dog kennel-like cages.

The worst came a month later when protest-ers tried to clear the main bridge into the camp that had been blockaded with burned cars and debris since the summer. They faced rubber bullets and tear gas, but also water cannons that drenched them in the freezing cold. Twenty-six were badly injured. A miracle, perhaps, that no one got killed.

What compelled Vernon Benjamin to visit Standing Rock? He was neither a traveler nor a protester. Aside from visits to his daughters' families in Kentucky and Ohio, he rarely left his beloved Hudson Valley except to venture farther out into New York State. He'd been born and raised and still lived in Saugerties. He'd explored the region in depth for his two-volume *History of the Hudson River Valley*, but had never felt the urge to Go West, Young Man! He'd never even taken a true vacation.

As for politics, he was passionate about his causes. For more than forty years he'd worked within the system as a journalist, a legislative aide in Albany, even as the town supervisor of Sauger-ties for a term. Not for him protest placards or one-note slogans. Democrats? Republicans? He had friends on both sides. Yet at 70 he loaded his pickup with thirteen bales of hay to feed horses and other supplies for the protesters, and set out for Standing Rock.

Trump's election had shaken him badly. He feared the country had given in to a dark and bitter spirit as Britain had by voting for Brexit. As a veteran environmentalist he was also well versed in the Hudson Valley fights over fracking, oil trains, barges, and pipelines. No one needed to convince him the Water Protectors were fighting for a worthy cause. Most of all, he felt a deep and abiding respect for Native Americans. He'd fought for their causes in Albany. He'd researched their history in the Hudson Valley. Three years earlier he'd been deeply involved in supporting a Two Row Renewal Campaign in which Haudenosaunee canoeists paddled 150 miles from central New York down the Hudson River to the United Nations to call attention to a treaty signed 400 years earlier. Benjamin followed their journey upriver and down. When they reached Saugerties, he welcomed them at the waterfront. When Standing Rock hit the news, he may have seen himself as an ambassador representing his beloved Hudson Valley who'd bring a show of support.

He reported on his trip in emails to his Go-FundMe supporters and in dispatches to local papers. On Thanksgiving Day his emotions reached a peak of eloquent rage. In the *Woodstock*

Times he wrote about the small town of Cannon Ball near the encampments:

"November 24 — I go to Cannon Ball in North Dakota, to the sacred fire of the Oceti and the seven nations of the Sioux, where the road is blocked by burned wrecks and the protesters are falling before water cannons and two-inch plastic bullets that can knock a man down.

"I am one with America in my ride, and yet I am far away from my family in Kentucky and Ohio, toward whom I nod as I pass by. I drive on the day when the Pilgrims gave thanks for the safety the protectors gave them in the strange new land in the past, just before they killed them all. They were a people like the Oceti, a people who welcomed the strangers to the best that they had, who were honest without laws, who had no jails or poorhouses, who were free from the religious animosities that have poisoned the rest of us, a people who had no love of money and who never fought a battle against the white man except on their own ground. As they are doing today, on their own ground.

"Will the pipeline be unbroken in another 50 years? Where has the conscience of America gone? I go to walk among its broken shards."

A historian, Benjamin knew he was driving out to history in the making, one of the most galvanizing protests of our times. That same Thanksgiving Jane Fonda hosted a turkey dinner for 500 in Cannon Ball. As she then wrote for *Time* magazine, "What is happening at Standing Rock is historic. This is the first time since Little Big Horn in 1876 that Oceti Sakowin have come together in peace as one family." At the camp she admired the ceremonial fires, the sweat lodges, the kindness. "I have never been hugged so much in my life."

A few weeks later another visitor, a young activist and bartender from the Bronx, was deeply impressed by what she saw. She realized that it wasn't enough to get angry over politics. You had to act. The day she left Standing Rock Alexandria Ocasio-Cortez got a call from a fledgling group called Brand New Congress asking if she'd consider running for office. She returned home to become one of the most charismatic political leaders of our time.

Vernon Benjamin had a different experience. What's striking about "Crossing Divides," which he worked on for four years after his trip, is that he leaves out the larger story of Standing Rock. His trip turned into a journey into himself. The biggest divide he crossed was between Vernon Benjamin, the veteran observer of life as a journalist, legislative aide, and historian, and Vernon Benjamin, who at 70 now wanted to act upon his passionate convictions. As he later wrote, "Dauntless into the maelstrom of America I ride, but this is no mission for God or for mom, as were my missions in the past. I do not have the comfort of home to protect me. I am frightened, but I go alone."

You are about to read what he learned.

CROSSING DIVIDES
ONE

When I dropped into the Oceti Sakowan camp on a quiet Monday after Thanksgiving in 2016 a strangely overcast sky that shadowed me across North Dakota had already arrived. I could feel the storm coming on, two days sooner than I expected, and I knew that I was not long for this place given how shabbily I was attired for winter. The fog hovered about twenty feet over the vale. Two men shared a laugh while directing me to a corrugated shack, where a thin older man, also jovial looking, stepped forward.

"I have supplies for the Oceti camp," I said.

"For who?" He flailed his arms and half laughed as he spoke, so I repeated my words and asked for their council fire.

"Their wwhhaaatt?" He drew out the word like a funnel, and I realized he was messing with me a bit, sharing a quiet joke with somebody over there. That was fine. I looked like a pipeline worker in my pickup and baseball hat, and wondered how many of those fifth columnists were already here. I repeated my request. He motioned to a flat corrugated roof off the lane to the right. The council fire was over there, "that metal roof," he said. Talk to the young people standing outside.

I inched my truck into the narrow, muddy lane until I was sure of the tires, and entered the camp, a large and casual mix of makeshift habitats and domiciles — tents, yurts, plywood make-dos, tin-topped sheds with stovepipes protruding, numerous sturdy teepees spread across the narrow valley, many with wisps of smoke rising, much of it cluttered in small communities amid signs and flags of various nations and the principle they stood for: *Mni Wiconi* — Water Is Life. The paths were rimmed with pickups, cars, trailers, RVs, all of it lying in a white silence. The signs proclaimed Indigenous sovereignty, warriors standing with the water, challenges to the copper-hearted barbarians, requests for privacy. Nothing moved except an occasional person, heavily clothed against the cold, walking slowly and deliberately under the fog.

I came to the shack where a young man and woman waited. They wore black snowmobile coveralls and small "Security" badges that gave me a sense of relief. The man had a serious aspect, enough to make me imagine a warrior galloping across a death-white field — and immediately I winced at characterizing someone from notions out of my adolescent past. I explained that I had "a load of supplies" and wanted to find how best to dispose of them for the community.

I gave them a small bag of chocolate bars made especially for the trip. "And this!" I said, and grimaced again at appearing to bribe some unaware innocents with candy just to get my way. I hastily explained the sentiment behind the chocolates and how the ingredients were related to the Oceti cause. They were created by Rae Stang of Lucky Chocolates in Saugerties, New York, and included slips on each box ("Standing Rock Bark") announcing the ingredients:

chocolate, for love and support
organic ginger, for warmth
organic cranberries, for stamina
organic sunflower and pumpkin seeds, for power
organic almonds, for strength
sea salt, for replenishment of tears

Fifty one-pound boxes, a thousand dollar retail donation that Rae made overnight after learning that I was going to Standing Rock.

"Tastes pretty good," the young man said, and gave a piece to his companion. She was a beautiful young woman, round-faced with soft, friendly eyes — both of their cheeks were Christmas-red with the chill — and when she smiled I lit up inside. They spoke intimately to each other, "honey" and "sweetie" and other terms of endearment, and I realized they were a young, married couple, instead of the brother and sister I first imagined.

He checked the hay under the tarp. I felt that what little I had — the hay, the Standing Rock Bark, a Water Is Life banner, some mylar blankets, sleeping bags and heavy covers, half a dozen pair of Tibetan socks, a bag of warm knitted gloves and hats, a butane stove with extra fuel, several large containers of coffee and gallons of water, and a few other smalls — all of it seemed so hopelessly inadequate to me.

They talked a bit and then he said, "We will go down to the new tent."

I looked around me and felt an enormous satisfaction that I was here and in a very small way I was helping. Yet at the same time I was struck by the knowledge that, regardless of the weather, I did not belong here.

TWO

That was a strange revelation for me, given the 1,700 miles I had traveled and my own personal history and beliefs regarding the original peoples of America. I had come into North Dakota quietly the day before under the cover of that same high fog in a frowning sky. After leaving Fargo, the two-hundred-mile drive across the state traversed a vast black dirt area of large neat farms mottled here and there by stands of birch and firs, a silent landscape of houses, barns, and silos waiting for the winter winds; and the wires of power in the distance crossing the landscape along with me like independent travelers carrying their own precious cargo. Now and then a farm industry outlet — tractor and small equipment sales, processing operation, a mini-mall — drew a few houses into a little community. I knew I wasn't in my world anymore when I passed a sign that read "Continental Divide" and realized that I was indeed entering the wild, wild West. Oh, Mom, look at me now!

At fifty miles from Bismarck and already late afternoon and a cold rain come to join me, I decided against going into the camp after dark. I did not know the way after leaving Bismarck's sister city, Mandan, and I feared the rumors that the police were giving supply vehicles expensive tickets returnable in the local courts. I didn't want to have to spend the money I was bringing to the Oceti on my own court expenses.

I found a hotel room in Valley City and talked with a cautious yet curious clerk who, after some coaxing, expressed her opinion ("Why don't they just move the pipeline?"). I saw that she was nervous, so I said I wouldn't tell, whereupon she smiled and gave me the best room in the house. The bartender downstairs was of a different persuasion. She disapproved of the talk against the Indians on Facebook, yet also sympathized with the families of local policemen who worried when their sons and daughters were called up for duty at "the troubles." She felt they were going to lose the argument anyway so what was the point of the protest after all?

Then she said: "Why don't they just move the pipeline?" She moved on to another customer.

My neighbor at the bar was a man in his thirties on a two-day layover because of the weather. He piloted a Cessna 182, inspecting the pipelines at 500 feet elevation between Iowa and Canada, and hadn't had an incident in six years on the job. These days he paid particular attention to the farmers who were laying tiles to protect against erosion from the winter winds, often near a pipeline. He and his colleagues maintained a regular system of communication with the locals by phone, email, and radio, and a good relationship had developed over the years. He worked with five other pilots out of a central hub in Iowa carrying out a round-the-clock surveillance of all of the lines. I recalled my days as a truck dispatcher and how that thin connection with the home terminal felt like a lifeline to many of my drivers. My companion could only sit and watch the weather; after a couple of days, when the real storm came, I thought about him and wondered if he ever got out of that Valley City hotel.

The news that night reported the consternation at the camp when the Army Corps of Engineers said the Protectors would have to abandon the site a week from Monday. The warning was tempered by an assurance that there would be no forced removal, but all the same they knew that the state, the National Guard, and the company would be pressing for a full evacuation by any means at their disposal. The Protectors, however, were busy preparing for a more aggressive enemy than anything man could dish out — the winter on its own brutal terms. They also wanted to ensure that the visitors who came in support were not jeopardized, and that was why my hosts decided to take me to the new tent when I arrived the next day.

His name was Juan, his wife was Toni. He told me that two nights earlier his father, one of the council chiefs, became frustrated by the actions of some other chiefs who denied blankets and other cold-weather support to visitors, claiming wrongly that they had no supplies. He decided on his own to establish a new area to store supplies for the visitors. Juan said they planned to "go into the city" the next day and buy the gear they needed. He hesitated and said they also had a need for money, but went no further; he was uncomfortable with the topic, and may have thought that I was poor as well.

He and Toni walked ahead, leading me down to a group of large tents not far from the entrance gate. We talked outside in the cold for a few minutes; my feet were already chilled. I was carrying over $2,000, but did not think twice about the money; I knew that whatever I did with the cash was bound to help in some way. I gave them the envelope before we went into the tent and said, Do with this what you wish; it is only meant to help. I had a personal card with my ID tucked in some pocket, but did not bother with that; my anonymity was my true identity.

I worried that the heavy rain the night before had spoiled the hay, but when I removed the tarp, everything was dry. The tent already had some goods in it, and my thirteen bales seemed so paltry and insignificant that I was embarrassed. I had not loaded more hay because I feared the wreck of the wind on the tarp as I crossed the country, and in fact I had to stop and adjust the cover several times en route. And there was something symbolic about the hay that transcended its paucity; it came from Kenny Snyder's ninth-generation farm on a hillside overlooking a small clove that Haudenosaunee and earlier aborigines — probably even the first Paleoindians to come our way — had walked over the centuries from the interior of New York into the central Hudson Valley.

"That's the furthest any of my hay has ever gone," Kenny said as we loaded it into my truck the week before.

The day before I left my home I prepared a slow cooker meat loaf and made seven large sandwiches with nice thick ciabatta bread. I would eat these while at the camp to ensure that I did not take anything from my hosts and could be self-sufficient while I was there. But once it was clear to me that I would not be staying, I gave the sandwiches to Toni and Juan. She opened one and began eating it, pulling Juan over and telling him to have one, too. I saw that they were both hungry and was glad that I had some nourishment other than the spiritual nourishment of the chocolates and the good will of a distant place to bring to them. My preparations had included emails to former colleagues at Marist College in Poughkeepsie, where I had been an adjunct lecturer, and the word got around; many sent cash for me to include in my donations, as did local friends I had contacted.

THREE

When I left my home early Thanksgiving morning, I was already two hours behind schedule. I worried that I might run into bad traffic in my passage along the Wilkes Barre ridges over to I-80 in Pennsylvania two hours later, but it was as quiet as a Sunday crossing the I-84 forests and, except for some trucks, I had clear sailing. I found a gruesome pleasure in the idea that I was taking gifts to the Indians on the day that the New England part of my culture celebrated the gift of life from them — a decade or two before they killed them off — and considered myself a part of the new thinking about our history with these people. I had done service to Native American causes as a legislative aide in New York in my past, and in writing about prehistory in my Hudson River Valley account, taking special pains to "know the new facts first," as Charles Olsen had admonished, and thought I did a good job at it.

Akwesasne was Mohawk Indian territory that straddled the St. Lawrence River near and partly through the city of Messina in northwestern New York. I was there in 1991 as an aide to Maurice Hinchey, a member of a state Assembly subcommittee on Indian affairs that came to hold hearings and support the traditionalists over the gaming troubles and the smuggling of cigarettes into Canada. Hinchey already had a history with these peoples for helping to browbeat Alcoa Aluminum into cleaning up the St. Lawrence around Akwesasne. Much of the small Indian nation on the American side included an archipelago of islands and a dizzying complex of dirt roads that rimmed the river in a bleak backwater landscape known as the Snye. A wily young smuggler in a fast boat with $100,000 in contraband could elude any of the seven police jurisdictions that patrolled this area during the troubles. A traditionalist who fought the casino and smugglers had been murdered — a man on the American side of the river killed by high-powered rifle fire from the Canadian side — and an advocate journalist was unfairly blamed, so the atmosphere was tense among the Indian factions and the police.

We took a yellow school bus ride through the Snye, passing homes of anti-casino leaders with bullet holes in the outer walls. The hearing was at the Native elementary school, where Chief Jake Swamp rendered a two-hour version of the traditional Haudenosaunee greeting to open the hearing. "That Jake, he never shuts up," Mohawk Chief Tom Porter joked for the community of young people who settled around him. The greeting was a thanksgiving prayer (which can take much longer) that was a moving experience that brought me closer to the Native sentiment, and when I witnessed Chief Porter give the greeting himself at Russell Sage College twenty years later (in half the time), I felt its true power emerge in Porter's gentle style. The hearings produced a record of the violence and difficulties over a casino siting and the incidence of cigarette smuggling, but little else in terms of a long-term New York State response; in fact, the state was engaged in court fights over land rights and trying to secure taxes for the cigarettes that were sold on the reservation. New York's history with the Haudenosaunee over the years was a deplorable one — one of the few states that never fully recognized federal jurisdictions and the independence of the Indian nations. Of course, none of this had the approbation of Assemblyman Hinchey and his colleagues.

I had always appreciated the notion of Montezuma's revenge, especially the gift of tobacco as a killing tool, and taking the money from the whites seemed appropriate when the casino option arose, but I was not a fan of casinos. The revenues from Indian ownership might settle a few scores, but for a spiritual people, casinos were the foreigner's totems that the traditionalists swallowed with appropriate bitterness. And early on the interest seemed purely venal on the part of some of the casino organizers. Now, a score of years of arguments behind us, the casino had settled in as a reasonable Indigenous response to American capitalism.

I think everyone understood that the traditional Indians would lose at Standing Rock, as they did with the gaming at Akwesasne and in almost all their confrontations with the exploiters, and the black snake would writhe, but, just as at Akwesasne during those troubles, a greater victory would emerge. Tom Porter moved his Mohawk community back to the Mohawk River, affirming the traditional ways in an embrace of their ancestral lands. The Haudenosaunee council fire at Onondaga blazed brighter and its spirit thrived in the effort to save and restore Onondaga Lake and assert the birthright of a proud people who never lost their traditions and whose land was never ceded. Just delaying the pipeline at Standing Rock was a victory, made all the more remarkable in the solidarity of more than two hundred original nations that came together under the common cause, and with them the bodies and spirits of thousands of non-Indigenous Americans who understood that the persistent cough of fossil fuels was killing the earth.

FOUR

My own feeling about the importance of carrying hay to the Oceti was reinforced by my getting there. This was another paradox for me when I realized I didn't belong. I bought a small CD player to listen to my own music on the way, but I never used it and instead kept flicking the truck radio channels to eavesdrop on the America I was crossing. One of the right-wing talk shows had a conversation between a host and a Southern guru on the ways in which Thomas Jefferson's America were degraded by the liberal talk. My mind raced through alternate readings and profoundly disturbing ways in which the words of the founders were so badly misinterpreted, yet I enjoyed the man's paternal voice — he was like a Franklin Roosevelt with drawl — as he preached his thinking and his ways. I let the radio channels drift after that; this wasn't about politics but about me trying to catch the themes of place in snippets of music and voice as background noise. Whatever came up on the next fast forward was good enough for me, and also helped me to dip into the great variety of the American scene more than any biased chatter I might hear.

I thought of my trip as a "Mission for Mom," since she and I shared a deep radicalism that was not true of the rest of the family. I had made up my mind to help Standing Rock in the summer, and was not concerned that it took until November to free up my schedule. I knew I needed to let it sink in, just as this narrative has over time. And when my truck dipped through the fabulous geology leading from I-81 to I-80 in Pennsylvania, I realized where I was going and why. The landscape reminded me of when I spent three months in the New York Geological Survey library in Albany doing my geology history research. A little old lady with a nice smile placed one after another of the books, texts, maps, and reports on Hudson Valley geology before me, some 180 references in all. Gradually, four or five hours at a clip, I developed an understanding of the complex forces that made up my valley and was able to complete my summary on the subject for my book, *The History of the Hudson River Valley*. The experience helped me to understand the powerful forces that were at work where the Appalachian Plateau yielded to the Great Valley more than a hundred miles away in Pennsylvania.

I came through a long downward curve between a pair of camel humps into an awesome view of the Great Valley. As I crossed a bridge that curved with the interstate, a ten-wheeler with a bright yellow trailer passed on my left. I happened to glance to the right as I strengthened my grip to accommodate the wind shear that the passing truck caused, and there appeared in my periphery a momentary landscape of exquisite beauty, a stretch of stream rimmed by low-hanging firs that caught me up in images of Thoreau and John Burroughs and a brief yet indelible moment of a past in which no highways or bridges existed and only the streams that brought life flowed through these natural climes. *Mni Wiconi.* The roar of the traffic disappeared; I was suspended in an epiphany of what I saw. The setting passed and I continued on, the force of the interstate vaulting me like an atlatl shaft into a stunning new geography at the same moment that I yearned to return to that place in space and time I had just left, into the living past that was now gone. The truck passed me by. Directly in front of me a juvenile bald eagle, its brown wings tucked tightly into torso, glided across the interstate into a small stand of trees on the highway's divide.

I continued, my thinking pregnant with a sense of a time that had no sense of time. From then on, I found myself referencing the Native American names and places that I passed, thinking how casually they were taken up by the trappers and settlers and made their own. One after another town and highway and hillside and stream names transported me into the sense of a past appropriated. I was reminded of the Indian notion that to take something's name is to take its identity and possess it. I smiled, knowing that these names were only place markers to guide the traveler: Indians never shared their personal, intimate identities with strangers. Those of my land were called *Muhhikanituck*, which meant the place with the waters constantly in motion or, loosely translated, the river that flows both ways. That was what the coastal Native told the seventeenth century Dutch when they asked; we who are outside the forest do not know them to this day in their true identity.

I so much appreciated the Pennsylvania interstate compared with New York's antiseptic Thruway because the divide between east and west lanes often remained as natural settings, small forest groups left standing as if to advertise this part of America for what it once was, a land undisturbed by the hand of man. The subsequent geological divides were also important for me. Passing from the Chesapeake watershed into the Susquehanna, I felt as if I had come full circle because the Susquehanna touched the Hudson watershed just fifty miles from my home. In Ohio I crossed the divide between the Great Lakes and Mississippi watersheds, and fifty miles shy of Bismarck, North Dakota, the surprise of the Continental Divide itself, 1490 feet elevation, when I passed a tractor trailer laden with black pipe while thinking of my mother.

On the second day of my trip, I reached the Mississippi and went a hundred miles out of the way to Mankato and its memorial to thirty-eight Sioux warriors hanged there in 1862, the largest mass execution in U.S. history. The warriors keened their death chants on the gallows when they died. Their names are listed on the memorial, which includes sculptures of an Indian brave and a large stone buffalo. The site was created in 1998 by well-meaning folks, yet precipitated a deep-seated divide within the wider southern Minnesota community that included farm families who had lost ancestors — whole families of them — in the massacres of that war.

I went to Mankato because Chief Gus High Eagle and his band of South Dakota braves had come through there twice, in their first Unity ride in 2010 and again with their beautiful horses on their way to support the Haudenosaunee in New York in 2013. Their first difficult early winter trek was recorded in a film that depicted the communities along the way helping them on their mission, taking them in from the biting cold during the terrible storm days, caring for their horses and sharing with the braves their food and hospitality. The braves were a proud young lot; one of them featured in the film later committed suicide over the desperation of his life back in South Dakota.

FIVE

I took a couple of pictures of Toni and Juan — I wanted to see their faces again — and left them at the tent. I turned into the Oceti camp and followed the allee of flags, more than two hundred banners of various nations that had come in support. The Oceti were the keepers of the council fire for the seven Sioux tribes, which made this location a fitting stand to wrestle the black snake, a place where all Indigenous nations could join in the solidarity of the seven. That was the most astonishing thing to happen here, so many thousands of original peoples coming into this unforgiving landscape with their different cultures and worlds to be with their brothers and sisters.

The place was also important as appropriated land, land that had been ceded to the Sioux in the Treaty of Fort Stanwix in 1851 and then taken by the strangers at a later time; it was considered sacred ground. So much of that treaty, the only one that America ever entered into as a defeated nation, was later abrogated, another hard stone for Sioux to endure in their Sisyphean struggle for justice. Here were just some of the flags of their sisters and friends: Swinobish Indian Tribal Council, Lummi Indian

Nation, Oglala Lakota, Sycuan Band of the Kumegaay Nation, Mni Wiconi of the Shenandoah Valley, Black Lake First Nation, South Fork Band of the Western Shoshone of Nebraska, White Mountain Apache Tribute — a magnificent Great Seal! — Muscogee Nation, Crow Creek Sioux Nation, Pueblo de San Felipe, Red Lake Nation, Hiawatha First Nation Mississaugas of Rice Lake, Alderville First Nation, Curve Lake First Nation, United Federation of Taino People, Redrum First Nation Warriors for the People, Spirit Lake Tribe, Winnebago Tribe of Nebraska, Commanche Nation Lords of the Plains, Salt River First Nation, Pyramid Lake Paiute Tribe, Soboba Band of Luiseno Indians, Calito Tribe, and on and on, a dazzling display of strength and beauty, one flag after another as far as eye could see.

I learned that the flags of the six nations of the Haudenosaunee stood in solidarity together on the far side of the camp. I wanted to know about the Haudenosaunee — some historians still call them the Iroquois — because, in addition to my Hinchey work, I had both small and large histories myself with those Mohawk Valley nations. On a writing assignment into the Genesee Valley, I spent time at the Mary Jemison gravesite with John Thomas, a local Seneca, and wrote a poem about her spirit hovering over those pines:

A child of the ocean, taken among them as
    one of their own,
she lived in the time of Handsome Lake
    among a loving people
who always made her welcome to the best
    they had,
who were honest without laws, without jails,
    without poor houses,
who never stole nor raised a hand against her,
who had no love of money, and never fought
    the white man
except on their own ground.

In my later history research, I came upon the Two Row Wampum, an agreement between Dutch and Mohawks overlooking the Hudson on the Tawasentha in 1613 that caused me to put aside my book and spend six months researching and writing an article on the topic. The Two Row, a sacred artifact of Haudenosaunee culture, is a belt of shell beads in two rows of purple on a bed of white, signifying the decision of these two peoples to proceed together in their canoes down the river of life, paddling in parallel, helping each other when needed but never crossing into the others' path or trying to dominate the other.

After my book appeared, and because of the interest my article generated, I was invited to Syracuse University to address a class on Native American issues. I began with the standard story of the evolution of the peoples of prehistory and the evisceration of their spirit in the encounter with the Europeans. Then I stopped and looked around the room at a cross-section of youths from different cultures. An anger came over me; I spent the rest of my time exhorting them to take up the cause themselves and work toward justice for original peoples everywhere. I felt surprise at the passion rising in me, and then immediately felt that my surprise was the real surprise for me: Why wasn't I as passionate all along? Where was passion at all in my life?

My thoughts spiraled into my youth and professional life as I realized that it was true: I had been living only halfway into life, a spectator rather than a participant whose education, religious history and work had placed me once removed from reality. Journalism accounted for some of it, of course; reporters are not supposed to be engaged in the news they write, only dispassionately to record it — and I was very good at that. Yet I found that after several years I could no longer distinguish my real self from the artificiality I had made of myself. After I quit my job, I realized over time that my dissociation from reality was much deeper than a collateral impact caused by work and instead developed from my childhood. I was advanced a grade in my Catholic elementary school, became immediately removed from my peer group and never assimilated well into any future relationships. On my return trip across America, I analyzed these feelings with every passing mile and concluded that I had gone through the motions of life — with school, with Hinchey, with my writing and my intellectual grasp of the history, with my passions about the Indigenous — with only a vague sense of commitment.

This conclusion was all the more striking for me since I thought I had Indian blood. I was a descendant, on my father's mother's side, of the Hudson River Palatines, the 1710ers as they were called, a group of three hundred High German families who were brought over by the British to work off their "debt" for the succor the British had given them in their escape from a homeland ravaged by the wars of Louis XIV. They were forced to boil tar and pitch from scrub pine to provide the British Navy with naval stores. The experiment failed and two years later the families were allowed to disperse. Most went northwest and established communities in the Schoharie Valley, where land had been promised them by a Haudenosaunee chief visiting their encampments in England. Some remained in the Hudson Valley and married among Dutch farm families who had preceded them, some made homesteads across the river with the manor lord, and some made it only to the foothills of the Catskills, at a divide where the Haudenosaunee entered the Hudson

Valley from Iroquoia, a small farming community tucked beneath a deep geological slash in the northeast face of the Catskill Mountains known as Platte Clove. My family, the Beckers, were among the latter group, and some within my grandmother Effie's memory married Oneida and Onondaga whose ancestors came down from the mountains to trade. We had nineteenth century tintypes of them in the attic.

But that ancestry did not come down to me, I later learned. Maybe that was it. Maybe my sympathetic connection with Native American causes was merely an extension of my wishing it so.

SIX

The 2013 Two Row Wampum event was an epic canoe trip from the heart of Onondaga in central New York through the 150 miles of the Hudson River estuary to the United Nations, the Natives crossing the divide that separated the forest from the newcomers. An appeal was made for New York State and the United States to "brighten" and renew the tarnished agreement and honor all treaties with original peoples. They were received at the UN with the diplomatic respect to which they were entitled, and Holland later issued an apology to the Haudenosaunee for the abuses they suffered under Dutch rule in the seventeenth century; but of course the United States and New York State remained silent.

I contributed to the anniversary event in ways that were special to me. I accompanied Maurice Hinchey — now a retired U.S. congressman — to Onondaga for the kickoff event in the spring of that year. When we arrived he was asked to join the opening processional by leading the visitors down one aisle while the Todadaho led the Natives down the other to the stage. He was both the symbolic and, as a former congressman, literal representative of the United States. Neither of us realized the full import of his role until he reached the stage and turned and saw the crowded auditorium on its feet, cheering and applauding. Later one of the speakers stepped up to relate the tragic history of how the Haudenosaunee were treated by New York — but at one moment while he spoke, he stopped and told the crowd that he needed to speak of "one among us" who broke that mold and always stood by the side of the Haudenosaunee: Maurice Hinchey. Maurice looked at me as if to ask what was going on, and of course I only vaguely grasped the meaning until we both turned to the audience and saw them once again on their feet, now turned toward him, applauding. We looked to the stage and in the rear of the group, sitting in his wheelchair, the aging former chief of the Onondaga, Irving Powless, was looking at Maurice and smiling; later we learned that he put the speaker up to it.

I helped draft a resolution in support of the campaign that twenty governments passed, including my own county, and when their flotilla arrived at my town, we welcomed them with a lunch of pizzas at the dock and showers for forty-six of the travelers at our nearby recreation center. The long hill outside the center was called Canoe Hill. My town symbol was designed in the 1950s by my father at the request of the then-town supervisor — a chief's profile in full headdress surrounded by the words Friendship, Man, Earth, Nation. The supervisor admired the painting my father did on a canoe he owned.

I also helped welcome Chief Gus High Eagle and the Unity Riders when they arrived in Woodstock in support of the Two Row, where another fine committee came together on their behalf. At Standing Rock, I saw the struggle with the black snake as exactly the same struggle that the Haudenosaunee endured over the decades when the parallel paths of sincerity and cooperation were breached, and that the South Dakota Sioux and Indians elsewhere were experiencing on a daily basis.

When I spoke with High Eagle, I unintentionally used the original name of the Haudenosaunee (which I do not use in this context out of respect for their privacy), and that prompted him to look me in the eye and confide fully in the progress that had been made until then. Later, forty miles downriver at a festival for the paddlers on the waterfront in Beacon, New York, I watched in admiration as High Eagle, Oren Lyons, and Pete Seeger stood together before the hundreds of Natives and visitors who came to witness the paddlers' arrival.

Chief Lyons, a man of great gentleness and good humor, was the Haudenosaunee representative to the United Nations and the international community. He was Maurice Hinchey's special guest on the floor of the New York State Assembly more than twenty years earlier, during the heady days when the Assembly subcommittee tried unsuccessfully to create the position of Native American "ambassador" or nonvoting member to that state legislative body. When Maurice escorted him onto the floor — a formal occasion reserved for visitors of special note — he introduced Oren as an Army paratrooper in Vietnam. The place erupted in cheers and a standing ovation. Years later, when Oren took me into the Haudenosaunee longhouse in his Onondaga homeland, I playfully remarked that I had had the privilege years before of "escorting the escortee" from our office to the Assembly chamber.

At Beacon, the three leaders joined in the songs of unity and justice on the round earth dais near the river that flowed both ways. I knew Pete also from my Hinchey days and joined him while he watched more of the performances. When we talked later I thought I'd have a little fun: I said that I wished he had sung my favorite Pete Seeger song that day.

"Which one is that?" he said.

"My Sweetheart's the Mule in the Mine," I said, a banjo ditty about a miner who chewed tobacco while riding his mule-drawn cart and spit the juice "all over my sweetheart's behind." Pete's wizened eyes sparkled and he smiled.

Later, as we walked along the waterfront together watching the paddlers arrive, he told me of his wife Toshi's passing the year before, with only their daughter and Pete there, and how quiet it had been. Pete died a year and a half later, and it since occurred to me that in the flat black vastness of time we lose our heroes — and they are only a very small number, and not from all generations, and often not the ones we expect — "to the lists," as the Greeks might say, where they become our icons and we are never left without them in the future manifestations of our needs and memories. Pete entered the lists in 2014 and is with us still; Maurice Hinchey and Gus High Eagle went there in 2017.

Recalling my thoughts about Pete as I passed across the Mississippi coming home, I wondered who would be our future icons. Would they have the same strength and resolve that Pete and Gus had, the same intensity that Maurice possessed? Would they take up the staff in whatever new and fabulous ways the need for new heroes possessed? And was it possible, by some chance, that one of the children walking the rain and snow-drenched fields of Oceti Sakowan that afternoon might be one of them? For me that was Toni and Juan.

SEVEN

On my return I stopped in South Bend, Indiana, to drop off a few bars of Rae Stang's Standing Rock Bark at a chocolate store I had heard about. I had a burger and chowder in a restaurant that served as a common gathering spot, and as I sat back I found myself across from a discussion group forming to talk about religion. The leader of the session was putting forth the notion that a formal church structure was not needed to pursue the important religious matters of modern times, and instead a "community group" convocation would suffice. I stifled a cynical thought that he might be feathering his own future nest, yet considered the conversation genuine. I felt like talking to them but could not form my thoughts well. Over the next couple of hours, as I headed for Ohio, I let the notion of what I might have said drift with the sounds of the highway into me.

I was heading home from Cannon Ball, North Dakota, where I had spent two and a half days talking quietly among new friends about the effort to stop the pipeline from crossing under sacred land. Those Natives with whom I spoke imparted the same sense of serious and genuine honesty as the voices I heard rise from the colonial documents in my history research, the soft voices of time rising from hundreds of years ago and a thousand miles away. In the seventeenth century whole societies were destroyed by the epidemics the Europeans brought and the insidious infection of rum, but in a much larger sense their entire society was eviscerated by the lure of the pelts and the trinkets they provided. Historian Calvin Martin termed it a form of apostasy, in which the spiritual self was rejected in the haste to enrich the corporal self. I'd say their soul was murdered instead, but whatever it was, when the beaver, the mystical earth brother, was killed in such numbers that, like the Indians, all but a handful were gone from the Hudson Valley just fifty years after Hudson came and went, an essential connection in the metaphysical relationship between man and nature was destroyed, the logical corollary arising in the destruction of the people themselves. The mechanism was the trade — the trinkets, the rum, the small and useful tools of the new culture coming into the old — brought into the New World by the newly capitalist Calvinist Dutch.

At Cannon Ball these thoughts returned to me. I felt that the religious structures of those Europeans were intimately tied to the creation of wealth, and nothing had changed since then. Generation after generation of their successors — we independent, go-ahead people with a confidence the size of a continent and a blindness that matched it — invested our destiny just as inimitably in the spirit of wealth as had the seventeenth century entrepreneurs, and just as it was with the Indians so it was with the western world today. The proof of it lay in the natural disasters of modern times — coming home from the Oceti it was the tornadoes and fires of Tennessee, the flooding of Florida, and rains of the Northeast, and the gentle white calamity of snowfall that fell at that moment at that one place only in all America, there at Cannon Ball, where the protectors remained to affirm spirituality over greed. We were the new apostates, and with our souls came the earth's destruction in the consequences of our greed. The dissociation that I felt — my absolute knowledge that I did not belong at Oceti Sakowan despite the references and touchstones of my past life — was another natural corollary, a byproduct of the world in which I existed. I did not respond to life because I was already dead; I had been dead all along, killed by insidious capitalism.

Almighty Dollar indeed, for the dollar infects all thinking in America these days: the racism, the immigrant hatred, the cynicism and foulness of the new order are the consequences of a sanctimoniously hallowed heritage that our capitalist past invented. Yes, we do need a new community of values, as a nation and as a civilization. We must examine ourselves and our essential spirit just as this South Bend group was doing, not to dethrone or deny religion or the world, but to repurpose the community of man in an embrace of the simplest of values, the ones that have been there all along for us to see and witness, the first peoples' notion of spirituality and nature sustenance.

That is what I would have said to these Christians.

VERNON BENJAMIN:
A LIFE

EARLY 1980s

In the broader world, Vernon Benjamin (1945-2022) is best remembered as the author of a two-volume magnum opus, *The History of the Hudson River Valley: From Wilderness to the Civil War* (2014) and *The History of the Hudson River Valley: From the Civil War to Modern Times* (2016), which took him twenty-plus years to research and write as he put twenty-thousand miles on his motorcycle, touring the valley to find the links between what we see today and what he learned from archives and museums. These books marry the writerly charm he'd honed as a local newspaper columnist with his vast curiosity about everything from the plate tectonics that shaped the valley's geology to daily life among Native Americans to the Hudson River School of painters to the brick industry, "the largest in the world," to whatever came next. Not until 9/11 "when two planes violated the Hudson River Valley's airspace" did he find the concluding point because he was already years late delivering his manuscript.

Over the course of this grand undertaking he published scholarly articles, lectured to historical societies and civic groups, and taught at Marist College. Known as tough grader, he was nonetheless held in awe by students as the guy who seemed to know everything there was to know about the Hudson Valley. He wasn't a trained historian, an academic veteran of classrooms, conferences, and journal citations. He was, instead, an independent spirit with an eclectic resume. He'd even registered as a lobbyist in Albany to advocate for acupuncturists. For the most part, he'd worked in small town journalism and in state and local government, but when Peter Mayer, the publisher of Overlook Books, asked if he'd write a history of the Hudson River Valley in the vein of Alf Evers' popular *The Catskills: From Wilderness to Woodstock*, Benjamin didn't hesitate. "I was born to do this!" he said. And so he was. The more he learned the more convinced he grew that our regional history was "a microcosm of American history." Of course, he got great help from friends, family, editors, and other historians. "Only my dog, Nick Baker, got fed up with it all, always wanting to take a walk when I wanted to work," he wrote in a preface, "but he got fattened up as well along the way."

NICK BAKER, FAITHFUL COMPANION

A lifelong Saugertesian, Benjamin grew up in an old house with a parlor stove and a front hedge he could climb up and hide in as a boy. His parents ran a flower shop. His father was a beloved figure, a grand marshal at parades, the mayor for a term, a truant officer in the schools, a little league coach, and the man who issued hunter training permits. His mother, more the pragmatist in the marriage, managed the store and the household. His two older brothers grew up to conventional careers, but Vernon may have felt a Bohemian calling from the start. In poems and short stories, he cast Saugerties in the late 1940s and 1950s as an almost mythical setting for a small-town American boyhood. There was fishing. ("Nothing like the smell of Mom's smelt in the frying pan those spring mornings.") There was the paper coating mill at the bottom of the hill where the noon whistle released the working men for half-hour lunch breaks at the nearby bars. ("They chased their beers with shots of hot sauce and argued about which bar made the best turtle soup.") And there were the trucks grinding up the hill. At the spot where drivers needed a free hand to shift gears, they tossed their cigarettes out the window. Vernon and his friends collected these prized butts to be tucked into the Kent packs they kept in their rolled-up T-shirt sleeves, as they played cards under the mulberry tree behind the laundry shop. In his adult life, Benjamin loved local lore so much he published *Toodlum Tales* for several years, a little journal named after a local hamlet.

VERNON WITH HIS GRAND-
FATHER IN THE LATE 1940s

FRESHMAN AT SAUGERTIES
HIGH SCHOOL

He graduated from Saugerties High School, then earned a B.A. in sociology from Siena College in Albany, and an M.A. in English literature from C.W. Post on Long Island. His thesis was on Jean Genet, an avant-garde French playwright of the 1950s and 1960s, and later in life Benjamin wrote several plays himself, including one about Benedict Arnold, the kind of complicated figure who fascinated him. A hero in the battles of Saratoga, Arnold then turned traitor when he took command of the fort at West Point. Benjamin, after finishing his encyclopedic histories, turned to fiction writing in short stories and novellas that often had elements of folklore and magical realism. One novella tells of a werewolf in New Amsterdam in

1643. In this account the monster morphs into a Native American figure called the Wendigo.

He wrote poetry throughout his life, or at least since high school when he composed poems to impress the girls. Later in life he'd send an email to friends with the heading: "Time for a poem." For example:

DARK AND LATE

It was dark and late.
I wrote a poem that made me
Afraid, so I left it

In the typewriter overnight.
When I got up the fear was gone,
And so was the poem.

After grad school, Benjamin entered the newspaper business at the *Register-Star* in Hudson, covering Red Hook and Columbia County, then he returned home as a "$5-a-story reporter" for the *Old Dutch Post* in Saugerties in the late 1970s. Even at that rate he did some investigative reporting into shady housing assessments. For five years, he also worked as a truck dispatcher at a cement plant a few miles upriver in Catskill, "the best goddamn dispatcher in New York State," according to a Teamster friend. At 36, he was diagnosed with Hodgkin's disease. Taking a biopsy, the oncologist "pulled a beautiful red killer pearl from my neck as I watched," he later wrote. A battery of drugs beat the cancer, but he never forgot the tenuous nature of life.

In 1982 he went to work in Albany as an aide to Assemblyman Maurice Hinchey, whom Benjamin had first known as a slick-haired, eighteen-year-old in a black denim jacket and jeans leading a pack of teens around Saugerties. At the time Benjamin was only twelve, so Hinchey was more familiar with his father, the school truant officer. Hinchey also worked at a cement plant when young, but he served in the Navy and returned to graduate from

BRUCE ACKERMAN'S CARICATURE OF
VERNON AS AN ALBANY LOBBYIST

SUNY New Paltz. In 1974, a landmark election year in the wake of Watergate, he beat the incumbent Republican, the first Democrat to win this seat in the Assembly since 1912. In Albany. he chaired the Environmental Conservation Committee and tackled such issues as toxic contamination at Love Canal, acid rain, and the influence of organized crime in waste hauling. As his top environmental staffer, Benjamin worked on many issues. Among his proudest accomplishments was advocating for the Hudson River Valley Greenway, a state agency to preserve and promote nature, history, and recreation in the 264 communities along the river.

He also ran for office himself. From 1982 to 1988 he served in the Ulster County legislature. From 1990 to 1992, he was the Saugerties town supervisor. It turned out he didn't have the forgiving temperament needed to be supervisor, but he had the foresight to acquire more land at Cantine Field for future soccer fields and a skating rink.

In 1992, Hinchey won a seat in Congress, so Benjamin returned home. Within a few years he began working on his history, but he never lacked for other activities. He was president of the Saugerties Public Library. He was a charter member of the Esopus Creek Conservancy that established a nature preserve on the creek. Early in his career he'd written a plan for restoring the Saugerties Lighthouse, and much later he helped lead plans to preserve Opus 40,

VERNON BEING CONGRATULATED BY HIS PARENTS, JOE AND ROSE BENJAMIN, UPON TAKING OFFICE AS SAUGERTIES TOWN SUPERVISOR IN 1990

Harvey Fite's bluestone sculpture park inspired by Mayan ruins. No slouch as a naturalist, he took biological assessment training to identify special ecological habitats for the town zoning and planning boards. He took Al Gore's *Inconvenient Truth* to heart and completed a leadership course inspired by the Academy Award-winning documentary to join 45,000 climate advocates around the world. He never stopped working for good causes.

In 1998 he returned to journalism as the editor of the *New Saugerties Times*, where he continued to write columns for another decade. In an obituary, Geddy Sveikauskas, his boss at Ulster Publishing, praised Benjamin for "his deep knowledge of his home town" that informed whatever he covered, be it sports at Cantine Field, a harbor seal seen at the lighthouse, or the VFW on Memorial Day. "Vern knew it all," he wrote, "And all the people, the people of Saugerties."

What the obituaries don't quite convey is the countless hours Benjamin spent at his keyboard, writing newspaper columns, government reports, magisterial histories. He honed his work. He cared about his words. He was buried at the Blue Mountain Cemetery in June 2022, but his writing often feels as fresh as if was written yesterday. The Standing Rock protests may have ended, but there will be another and another so long as global warming pummels us with downpours, floods, heat waves and skies with the smoke from distant forest fires. Until the end of his life, Benjamin shared the story of his efforts to intervene to push history ever so slightly in a better direction. He can still be our guide today and for generations to come.

ACKNOWLEDGMENTS

My gratitude to Suzanne Bennett, who introduced me to this essay; to Mary McNamara, Sarah Mecklem, and Mike Saporito, who oversee Vernon Benjamin's papers and shared wonderful stories about him; to Stacey Butcher and Rachel Bingham, his daughters who've given enthusiastic permission to publish *Crossing Divides*; to Rob Brill, who edited the manuscript; to Jessika Hazelton, who designed this book; to Weston Blelock, who distributes Bushwhack Books and offers crucial advice and support for all of our projects; and to Vernon Benjamin, whose essay brought all of us together to keep his memory alive.

Will Nixon

ABOUT WILL NIXON

Will Nixon started Bushwhack Books with Michael Perkins in 2009. Together they published *Walking Woodstock: Journeys into the Wild Heart of America's Most Famous Small Town*, *The Pocket Guide to Woodstock*, *The Woodstock Flaneur: A Saunterer's Intimate Portrait of the World's Most Famous Small Town*, and other collections of poetry and musings. Michael Perkins died in 2022, but the press continues to publish good writing from this region.